FRANCIS FRITH'S

HAYWARDS HEATH

LIVING MEMORIES

WILFRID JACKSON moved to Haywards Heath in 1973 after living in London. He is a Blue Badge Guide for South East England, the Heart of England and London. Currently he is Chairman of the South East England Guides Association as well as serving on the Executive Council for the Guild of Registered Tourist Guides (the national organization for Blue Badge Guides). He is also a City of London guide and a qualified trainer with the Institute of Tourist Guides. When time permits his other interests include antiques, wine and visiting art galleries.

FRANCIS FRITH'S
PHOTOGRAPHIC MEMORIES

HAYWARDS HEATH

LIVING MEMORIES

WILFRID JACKSON

First published in the United Kingdom in 2004 by
Frith Book Company Ltd

Limited Hardback Subscribers Edition 2004
ISBN 1-85937-912-5

Paperback Edition 2004
ISBN 1-85937-913-3

British Library Cataloguing in Publication Data

Francis Frith's - Haywards Heath Living Memories
Wilfrid Jackson

Frith Book Company Ltd
Frith's Barn, Teffont,
Salisbury, Wiltshire SP3 5QP
Tel: +44 (0) 1722 716 376
Email: info@francisfrith.co.uk
www.francisfrith.co.uk

Printed and bound in Great Britain

Front Cover: **HAYWARDS HEATH,** *South Road c1950* H252004
Frontispiece: **HAYWARDS HEATH,** *South Road 1954* H252012

*The colour-tinting is for illustrative purposes only, and is not intended
to be historically accurate*

CONTENTS

FRANCIS FRITH
VICTORIAN PIONEER

FRANCIS FRITH, founder of the world-famous photographic archive, was a complex and multi-talented man. A devout Quaker and a highly successful Victorian businessman, he was philosophical by nature and pioneering in outlook.

By 1855 he had already established a wholesale grocery business in Liverpool, and sold it for the astonishing sum of £200,000, which is the equivalent today of over £15,000,000. Now a very rich man, he was able to indulge his passion for travel. As a child he had pored over travel books written by early explorers, and his fancy and imagination had been stirred by family holidays to the sublime mountain regions of Wales and Scotland. 'What lands of spirit-stirring and enriching scenes and places!' he had written. He was to return to these scenes of grandeur in later years to 'recapture the thousands of vivid and tender memories', but with a different purpose. Now in his thirties, and captivated by the new science of photography, Frith set out on a series of pioneering journeys up the Nile and to the Near East that occupied him from 1856 unti 1860.

INTRIGUE AND EXPLORATION

These far-flung journeys were packed with intrigue and adventure. In his life story, written when he was sixty-three, Frith tells of being held captive by bandits, and of fighting 'an awful midnight battle to the very point of surrender with a deadly pack of hungry, wild dogs'. Wearing flowing Arab costume, Frith arrived at Akaba by camel sixty years before Lawrence of Arabia, where he encountered 'desert princes and rival sheikhs, blazing with jewel-hilted swords'.

He was the first photographer to venture beyond the sixth cataract of the Nile. Africa was still the mysterious 'Dark Continent', and Stanley and Livingstone's historic meeting was a decade into the future. The conditions for picture taking confound belief. He laboured for hours in his wicker dark-room in the sweltering heat of the desert, while the volatile chemicals fizzed dangerously in their trays. Back in London he exhibited his photographs and was 'rapturously cheered' by members of the Royal Society. His reputation as a photographer was made overnight.

VENTURE OF A LIFE-TIME

Characteristically, Frith quickly spotted the opportunity to create a new business as a specialist publisher of photographs. He lived in an era of immense and sometimes violent change. For the poor in the early part of Victoria's reign work was exhausting and the hours long, and people had precious little free time to enjoy themselves. Most

calibre of Roger Fenton and Francis Bedford. In order to gain some understanding of the scale of Frith's business one only has to look at the catalogue issued by Frith & Co in 1886: it runs to some 670 pages, listing not only many thousands of views of the British Isles but also many photographs of most European countries, and China, Japan, the USA and Canada - note the sample page shown on page 9 from the hand-written Frith & Co ledgers recording the pictures. By 1890 Frith had created the greatest specialist photographic publishing company in the world, with over 2,000 sales outlets - more than the combined number that Boots and WH Smith have today! The picture on the next page shows the Frith & Co display board at Ingleton in the Yorkshire Dales (left of window). Beautifully constructed with a mahogany frame and gilt inserts, it could display up to a dozen local scenes.

people had no transport other than a cart or gig at their disposal, and rarely travelled far beyond the boundaries of their own town or village. However, by the 1870s the railways had threaded their way across the country, and Bank Holidays and half-day Saturdays had been made obligatory by Act of Parliament. All of a sudden the working man and his family were able to enjoy days out and see a little more of the world.

With typical business acumen, Francis Frith foresaw that these new tourists would enjoy having souvenirs to commemorate their days out. In 1860 he married Mary Ann Rosling and set out on a new career: his aim was to photograph every city, town and village in Britain. For the next thirty years he travelled the country by train and by pony and trap, producing fine photographs of seaside resorts and beauty spots that were keenly bought by millions of Victorians. These prints were painstakingly pasted into family albums and pored over during the dark nights of winter, rekindling precious memories of summer excursions.

THE RISE OF FRITH & CO

Frith's studio was soon supplying retail shops all over the country. To meet the demand he gathered about him a small team of photographers, and published the work of independent artist-photographers of the

POSTCARD BONANZA

The ever-popular holiday postcard we know today took many years to develop. In 1870 the Post Office issued the first plain cards, with a pre-printed stamp on one face. In 1894 they allowed other publishers' cards to be sent through the mail with an attached adhesive halfpenny stamp. Demand grew rapidly, and in 1895 a new size of postcard was permitted called the court card, but there was little room for illustration. In 1899, a year after Frith's death, a new card measuring 5.5 x 3.5 inches became the standard format, but it was not until 1902 that the divided back came into being, so that the address and message could be on one face and a full-size illustration on the other. Frith & Co were in the vanguard of postcard development: Frith's sons Eustace and Cyril continued their father's monumental task, expanding the number of views offered to the public and recording more and more places in Britain, as the coasts and countryside were opened up to mass travel.

Francis Frith had died in 1898 at his villa in Cannes, his great project still growing. The archive he created continued in business for another seventy years. By

The handwritten ledger at top left reads approximately:

```
5
6      .      St Catherine's College                    +
7      .      Senate House & Library           +
8                                          +
9      .      Gerrard Hostel Bridge    +  +  + +
30     .      Geological Museum            +
1      .      Addenbrookes Hospital        +
2      .      St Mary's Church             +
3      .      Fitzwilliam Museum, Pitt Press &c  +
4                                          +
5    Buxton, The Crescent                     +
6            "    The Colonnade               +
7            "    Public Gardens              +
8                                             +
9    Haddon Hall, View from the Terrace       +
40   Miller's Dale                            +
1    Bakewell, Bridge &c.                     +
2            "    Footbridge                  +
3            "    Church                      +
4            "          Interior             +
5    Matlock Bath, The High Tor               +
6            "    On the Derwent              +
7            "          Brunswood Terrace     +
8            "    Cliffs &c                   +
9
```

1970 it contained over a third of a million pictures showing 7,000 British towns and villages.

FRANCIS FRITH'S LEGACY

Frith's legacy to us today is of immense significance and value, for the magnificent archive of evocative photographs he created provides a unique record of change in the cities, towns and villages throughout Britain over a century and more. Frith and his fellow studio photographers revisited locations many times down the years to update their views, compiling for us an enthralling and colourful pageant of British life and character.

We are fortunate that Frith was dedicated to recording the minutiae of everyday life. For it is this sheer wealth of visual data, the painstaking chronicle of changes in dress, transport, street layouts, buildings, housing, engineering and landscape that captivates us so much today. His remarkable images offer us a powerful link with the past and with the lives of our ancestors.

THE VALUE OF THE ARCHIVE TODAY

Computers have now made it possible for Frith's many thousands of images to be accessed almost instantly. Frith's images are increasingly used as visual resources, by social historians, by researchers into genealogy and ancestry, by architects and town planners, and by teachers involved in local history projects.

In addition, the archive offers every one of us an opportunity to examine the places where we and our families have lived and worked down the years. Highly successful in Frith's own era, the archive is now, a century and more on, entering a new phase of popularity. Historians consider the Francis Frith Collection to be of prime national importance. It is the only archive of its kind remaining in private ownership. Francis Frith's archive is now housed in an historic timber barn in the beautiful village of Teffont in Wiltshire. Its founder would not recognize the archive office as it is today. In place of the many thousands of dusty boxes containing glass plate negatives and an all-pervading odour of photographic chemicals, there are now ranks of computer screens. He would be amazed to watch his images travelling round the world at unimaginable speeds through internet lines.

The archive's future is both bright and exciting. Francis Frith, with his unshakeable belief in making photographs available to the greatest number of people, would undoubtedly approve of what is being done today with his lifetime's work. His photographs depicting our shared past are now bringing pleasure and enlightenment to millions around the world a century and more after his death.

HAYWARDS HEATH
AN INTRODUCTION

'HAYWARDS HEATH, this is Haywards Heath, the train now standing at platform three …' So goes the familiar announcement at one of the south-east's busiest railway stations. But what lies at the root of this town?

A document dated 1261 refers to 'Heyworth' (meaning 'a hedged enclosure') sited upon an expanse of heathland. By the 1500s it was recorded as 'Haywards Hoth'. There is an alternative romantic legend that a highwayman named Jack Hayward preyed on people travelling across this rather desolate heathland fringed by villages such as Cuckfield, Lindfield and Scaynes Hill. The heath was used as a place to muster troops during the English Civil War. However, it was not until the building and arrival of the railway that the seeds of the present town were sown.

The route that the London to Brighton railway was to eventually take was the result of 'nimbyism' from the residents of both Lindfield

Victoria Park, the Paddling Pool c1960 H252042

and Cuckfield, which were the principal stopping points on the coaching route from London to the coast. They lobbied for the track to be cut through the large expanse of heathland that separated the two communities. After all, what better solution could there be when those smoking noisy engines rushed through the area? The further away the better. Such was the energy and engineering skill of the railway builders that all the obstacles thrown in their path were duly overcome. Their most notable achievement was the building of the Balcombe tunnel and railway viaduct over the River Ouse, linking the higher ground of Balcombe with the Borde Hill estate lands which are located just to the north of Haywards Heath. The railway arrived in 1841. As with virtually all railway towns, the station became the nucleus for trade, and this was the embryonic beginning for Haywards Heath. Over the following 150 years it would evolve into the town that we know today.

In the 1850s the County Lunatic Asylum (later known as St Francis Hospital) was built on a high sandstone ridge to the south-east of the town, whilst in the 1860s the cattle market was established on the western edge of the railway station. In 1865 St Wilfrid's church was completed; it was built on the highest point in the town, and thus became a well-known landmark visible from the surrounding countryside.

Both commercial and residential growth continued, and was given extra impetus in 1933 when the railway was electrified. This led to nationally recognised retailers (Woolworth's, Boots and Sainsbury's) all opening in the town. By the late 1930s the cattle market was the twelfth largest in the country, but it closed in the early 1990s. The site was developed by Sainsbury's, whose large store is now easily seen from the trains passing nearby.

The population in the 1930s was over 7000; a proportion of the population commuted to London, a trend that has continued to this day. During the 1950s the Prime Minister, Harold Macmillan, used to travel from Haywards Heath (he lived at Birchgrove, a short drive away) as the commuting time was well under an hour for the 38-mile journey to London. Haywards Heath has also been able to capitalise on its close proximity to Gatwick Airport only 15 miles away - today it takes just 15 minutes on a fast train to get there.

There has been a continuous growth in population (it is currently about 23,000). There are a number of schools as well as a sixth-form college. The Dolphin Leisure Centre is extensively used by all members of the community, and the town council have been the driving force behind the successful twinning with Traunstein in Bavaria and Bondues in northern France. The Mid-Sussex District Council also has its main office here, whilst the County Council is based in Chichester.

The surrounding countryside is very attractive, and there are a number of National Trust gardens and estates in the immediate area (notably Wakehurst, Sheffield Park and Nymans). Other attractions include water sports at the nearby Ardingly reservoir, and the South Downs are just eight miles away. All the villages featured in this book are a short drive from Haywards Heath, and there are many examples of residents enjoying the village lifestyle whilst commuting to work by train via Haywards Heath. This has undoubtedly had an effect on the villages - some of the village businesses have been forced to close, for instance. This scenario is reflected throughout the length and breadth of the country as a whole: village schools and village shops are probably the most noticeable examples of disappearing amenities, though not the only ones, as we will see in this book. Each village has its own unique features, and I hope that this short tour will highlight them, and encourage readers to come and visit.

The names of the villages mentioned in this book denote their ancient lineage. Lindfield, and more importantly Cuckfield, wielded economic power as a result of the change from feudal to industrial wealth. By the 1600s, there were a number of wealthy families who had acquired large estates and whose names are still remembered today; the Sergison family is a prime example. Charles Sergison, having made his money from his Navy career, bought Cuckfield Park in 1691 and promptly displayed his newly created coat of arms with its dolphin crest. Almost 300 years later, in 1968, Cuckfield's final link with the Sergisons was severed when the estate was sold by Charles's descendant Captain Warden Brooke. When visiting Haywards Heath today, the reader will encounter a pub called the Dolphin (formerly called the Sergison Arms); the Dolphin Centre is the town's leisure complex; whilst Cuckfield's large secondary school is called Warden Park. The connections continue in road and housing estate names as well.

Geologically the area is within the Weald of Sussex - the name is derived from 'woodland'. This was part of what the Romans called the Forest of Anderida; it was later known as Andredswald by the Saxons, who then made small clearings in the woodland to create settlements. The heavy clay made travel difficult, especially in the damp and wet winter months. King Henry VIII laid the foundations of our navy, and a vast number of oak trees from this area were used to build the ships. Those vessels proved their worth in 1588, during the conflict with the Spanish Armada. As a result of the tree clearances, it was discovered that there were iron deposits here, and that they were commercially viable propositions for those willing (and financially able) to take the risk. In later centuries, agriculture became the dominant industry, but it was the arrival of the railway that really proved to be pivotal in the development of the area.

I hope that this short book will encourage many readers to come and visit both Haywards Heath and the surrounding villages. Space has dictated that only a brief caption is possible for each of the photographs; it may be surprising for visitors to see how much (or indeed little) change has taken place within the last half century. The route described in this book assumes that the visitor has arrived in Haywards Heath by train, and the tour starts from the railway station. The second part of the book is the briefest of introductions to the surrounding villages - a car will be needed for this tour. The route is anti-clockwise, starting from Lindfield, as it is the nearest village to Haywards Heath.

I trust that the reader will find this book enjoyable, as it has been a pleasure to recount my own 'living memories' of the town and the surrounding areas.

HAYWARDS HEATH

The Crossroads c1950 H252006

This photograph was taken from the platform of the railway station and emphasises the station's elevated position. The building on the left with the decorative heraldic badge between the upper windows is the Burrell Arms pub. Both the pub and the nearby shops were always useful to the increasing number of people who used the transport links here. The single-storey building standing on the right of the photograph is where the bus station was built in 1954. The traffic roundabout had only just been completed, hence the title of this photograph. This view has changed very little during the past 50 years.

*Commercial Square
c1960* H252038

The shops in the half-timbered parade have the advantage of a wider pavement for both pedestrians and deliveries, which no doubt the butcher Dewhurst found particularly useful.

◄ *Perrymount Road c1950*
H252586

We are looking towards Commercial Square. The road direction sign on the extreme left of the photograph denotes a crossroads junction, whilst attached to the next telegraph pole is a sign indicating the newly built roundabout (though illegible in this photograph, it is seen more easily in H252599, page 17).

◄ *Perrymount Road and Commercial Square c1950* H252002

Beyond the bus stop on the left-hand side is the Perrymount cinema, which also housed a dance hall and a café. It opened in 1936, and was very popular; it was also easy to get to, being a mere quickstep away from the railway station (off to the right of this view). Note the people under Edward Hodges' sunblind, which protected the garments displayed from becoming faded. Possibly some of the merchandise could only be purchased with the correct quantity of coupons, as wartime rationing had not yet ended.

detail of H252599 (below)

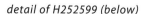

◄*Perrymount Road c1950*
H252599

The parked car is outside the Perrymount cinema, with Commercial Square beyond. Bradley & Vaughan are the estate agents based in the half-tiled building on the right edge of the photograph. This is a typical example of the local style of architecture dating from the 1870s. Notice the pattern formed within the tile-hung elevation - it is particularly attractive, and is complemented by the diamond-paned windows.
It was the lodge of St Clair, a large house that became a girls' school established by a Miss Stevens in about 1935.

▶ *Perrymount Road c1960* H252026

This is virtually the same view as H252002 (page 16-17), but how different it has become in the intervening ten years. The bus stop has been removed, as the bus station (built in 1954) is a busy terminus for the Southdown fleet of buses coming into Haywards Heath. Today, buses no longer terminate here; the site is ripe for redevelopment, and is currently for sale.

◀ *The Recreation Ground c1950* H252587

Created from the St Clair meadow, the recreation ground was an extremely popular venue, especially for cricket matches. The photograph shows a match in progress: the scoreboard is in the centre, with the sporting action out of camera shot to the left. Beyond the lamp standard in front of the parked car stands the then newly-built pavilion (its predecessor had suffered bomb damage in the Second World War). The mature trees provide shade for many of the spectators. Today, the adjacent site is now Clair Hall, opened in 1974 as an entertainment centre for films, plays and concerts, run by the local council.

▲ *The Recreation Ground c1950* H252010

In this quintessentially English scene, one can almost hear the sound of bat hitting ball, followed by the ripple of applause from the knowledgeable spectators. The grassy bank upon which some of the spectators are reclining helps to give a better view of the game.

◄ *The Recreation Ground c1950* H252588

This is another view of the same cricket match. The two men in the foreground are wearing military uniforms and are engrossed in conversation. They could be comparing their relevant military experiences, as compulsory conscription had not yet been repealed. The gentleman wearing cricket whites, walking on the higher path away from the camera, could be one of the players.

The Recreation Ground c1950 H252003

This attractive children's play area is set amongst pine trees next to the cricket pitch. The children in this photograph seem to be really enjoying themselves. The central swing boat was popular with younger children, and the little girl in the centre seems to be anxiously waiting her turn. The couple pushing the pram are possibly keeping an eye on the cricket as well as admiring the baby.

◄ *Perrymount Road c1950*
H252596

This photograph successfully shows the long incline of Perrymount Road. The bus coming up the hill would have already passed the recreation ground. The trees on the left have now been replaced by large multi-occupied office blocks, whilst those on the right shield the grounds of Jireh House; the house was demolished, and a development of flats was built on the site.

Perrymount Road c1965 H252068

The street lighting has been upgraded, though the gradient of the road still forced the cyclist to dismount to push his bike. The houses on the left were demolished to make way for an office block, whilst beyond the maisonettes on the right is a glimpse of the then new residential development of Jireh Court. The 1960s were an important period of expansion in Haywards Heath, and central locations for either commercial or residential developments were much in demand.

▶ *Jireh Court c1965* H252066

This is one of the major examples of 1960s residential architecture built in Haywards Heath. Location was key to the success of this development, as it lies between the main shopping areas of the Broadway and South Road, and yet only a short walk from the railway and bus stations. It proved ideal for commuters who worked in London, Croydon, Gatwick, Crawley or Brighton.

◄ *The Broadway c1950* H252597

Viewed from the raised footpath, the summit of Perrymount Road merges into the Broadway. The Broadway cinema is the large white 1930s-style building on the right of the photograph; it opened in 1932, and stood here for 20 years. It was then replaced by J W Upton & Sons, a furniture store, which in turn was demolished in 1987. The site is now an office complex for Lloyds Bank.

► *The Broadway c1960*
H252030

Looking southwards, this photograph gives an indication of the many businesses along this aptly named road. The furniture store and removals (right) is the family firm of J W Upton & Sons, whilst next door is Aunties, a sweet shop cum tobacconists, as we can see from the advertising boards immediately outside on the pavement. This part of the Broadway has altered little, and the buildings (though not the occupants) are recognisable today.

▶ *The Broadway c1965*
H252067

Virtually all the buildings on the right hand side of the photograph are still recognisable today, though the occupants have certainly changed, whilst the building on the left is the Midland Bank, now HSBC, and is still here. Both terraces have wide pavements in front, and the road is still wide enough for the cars to park on both sides.

The Broadway 1958 H252024

This photograph looks northwards. The Broadway also has a branch of the National Provincial Bank (third from the right) next to the post office, leading on to a greengrocer's, an optician's and a ladies' hairdresser amongst others. It is odd that the street lighting is only on the left side of the road, supported by the telephone poles.

The Broadway c1950
H252005

The young men on their bicycles are engrossed in conversation. The man on the left was definitely following the latest cycling fashion: note the drop handlebars on his bike. The attractive hanging sign of a man wearing a mask and pointing a pistol probably refers to the highwayman Jack Hayward, after whom Haywards Heath is possibly named. It was later removed, as we can see in photograph H252024 of 1958, page 24.

The Broadway c1950
H252584

Looking northwards, this photograph shows two-way traffic running the whole length of the Broadway (this is not the case today). The arched-roofed building on the right-hand side is the site previously used by the Coventry Motor Works, but by the 1950s it was one of several sites used by Caffyns, the countrywide car dealership business; its main site in the town is now on the western side of the railway station.

The Broadway c1960 H252059

A lot has happened in the space of just ten years since No H252584 (above) was taken. New street lighting has been installed, and although Caffyns are still here, there is a new Seeboard (electricity) showroom next door. Both businesses have now moved. Caffyns garage was demolished and replaced in the 1980s by a small parade of shops with offices above, whilst a business equipment supplier is currently based in the former electricity showrooms. The road heading off to the right leads to St Wilfrid's Church, and not unsurprisingly is called Church Road.

St Wilfrid's Church and the School c1950
H252001

Built in 1857, the school was originally known as the Chapel School; it was re-named St Wilfrid's School only after the church beyond had been built in 1865. Church Road follows the incline on the left. Built on the highest point, the church replaced a windmill. The school duly expanded, and the original building has had a succession of different uses - it is now a restaurant.

The Christian Science Reading Room c1960 H252056

After St Wilfrid's School had vacated these premises, the Reading Room was established and stayed here until the 1990s, when the Zizzi restaurant opened. Situated at the end of the Broadway, the restaurant is one of many that have become established here during the past decade. Other eateries include Café Rouge, Orange Square, and several independent restaurants serving Indian and Chinese cuisine.

▶ *South Road c1950*
H252009

This photograph was probably taken on a Saturday afternoon when it was possibly the only time in the working week when couples and/or families could go shopping together. It certainly would not be a Sunday, as no shop would be open for business. Society was becoming more affluent - note the number of private cars in this picture.

◀ *South Road c1965* H252065

South Road is the main shopping area in Haywards Heath. The shops are in the short parade on the left-hand side leading to St Wilfrid's churchyard, whilst offices occupy most of those buildings on the right - they adjoin Victoria Park, the largest open space in central Haywards Heath.

South Road c1950
H252004

The number 29 bus from Lewes is probably on the final part of its journey into Haywards Heath. Note the men on their bicycles and their clothes - only one of them is not wearing a tie. The building on the extreme right is the fire station. In 1961 the fire service moved to purpose-built premises near Commercial Square, and this building was demolished in 1981. Victoria Gate (shops with offices above) now stands on the site. On the left of the photograph, the parade of shops remains recognisable today, though the proprietors have changed.

South Road c1960
H252033

The road traverses a ridge, as we can see in this photograph. Deliveries to these shops would be from the access road at the rear of the terrace, though one lorry driver has decided to double-park in the main road. There are no road markings, and there does not appear to be a problem finding a space to park.

▶ *South Road c1950*
H252594

Though slightly
obscured by the
sunblind, there is one
shop in this parade
that is still here today
(2004). This is
Baldwin's, selling
household linens,
established by Edwin
Baldwin in 1935 when
this terrace was built.
This is one of the very
few shops that still
observe half-day
closing - each
Wednesday it closes
at 1pm.

◀ *South Road 1954*
H252012

Most of the national
retailers (Woolworth's,
Boots and Sainsbury's)
came to Haywards Heath
in the 1930s. The
electrification of the
railway certainly helped.
One shop is being
painted, perhaps a new
business starting up. This
is a prime spot, next door
to Woolworth's, with
Boots on the extreme
right of the picture.

▲ *South Road c1955* H252011

Sited on the Haywards Road junction, the white building on the extreme right is Lloyds Bank; this building was later demolished, but Lloyds are still on the same site. The shop with the flagpole (on the left-hand side of the road, just beyond the taller parade of shops) is George Hilton & Son, a furniture and furnishing store. George Hilton arrived in Haywards Heath from Hastings in 1882, and started a cabinet making business. By 1887, he was trading from this spot, though the building was not the same one we see here. He died in 1938. The site was re-developed, and the Orchards shopping centre was opened there in 1982.

▲ *South Road c1955* H252013

The projecting sign of Boots (centre) certainly helped to advertise its presence. Other nationally recognised names here include Freeman Hardy & Willis, WH Smith and Timothy Whites (on the extreme right). The number 84 bus seems to have a clear run; it need not be too concerned about the sole road marking, 'No Parking', at the Haywards Road junction.

▼ *South Road 1958* H252016

What a difference from H252011, on page 35! Look at the number of cars - no wonder road markings had been introduced. Most if not all of these cars would have been made in Britain, and may have been purchased through one of the town's car dealerships, Caffyns, Wadham Stringer or Dinnages.

▶ *South Road c1965*
H252060

South Road is the main route used for through traffic, which is why we can see a petrol tanker (centre left) going though the shopping area. This route is still used today, though there are plans for a bypass to the south of the town.

◀ *South Road c1950*
H252591

There is activity on the number 89 bus - passengers have come shopping. Currys, the electrical retailers, are on the extreme left of the photograph. Household goods such as washing machines and electric irons were just becoming more widely available, but at a price. No wonder that the shiny lettering and the black background attracted customers. It was an invitation to be part of the modern world of electric domestic appliances.

▶ *South Road c1950* H252593

Currys are at the far (west) end of the parade, whilst its counterpart at the east end (right) is the Fifty Shilling Tailors. This was where men could buy a suit, either outright or on hire purchase. On offer would have been suits made from traditional wool, or possibly from one of the then newly manufactured man-made materials. The money of the time was pounds, shillings and pence, with 20 shillings to a pound and 12 pennies to a shilling; a fifty-shilling suit would cost £2.50 in decimal currency. The early 1950s were times of scientific innovation, with new technology being used in the manufacture of both clothing and household goods. Virtually all these products would have been made in Britain. Could the driver of the car be described as 'middle of the road'?

South Road c1950
H252592

All the men in this photograph are wearing suits, so it is no wonder that the Fifty Shilling Tailor did a lot of business, It was the accepted mode of dress, particularly for work. Virtually all of the buildings in this photograph have been replaced; today the Orchards Shopping Centre is on the left, whilst on the opposite side of the road are currently Barclays Bank, Halfords and Robert Dyas.

South Road c1960 H252061

George Hilton's business (extreme left) had expanded across the road to the newly built brick building on the right of the photograph. It housed their furnishing departments (selling curtain materials, china, glassware, and so on) and was a magnet for shoppers. Imported goods were becoming more widely available, and people were becoming more affluent; money was available to spend on the home, the car or going abroad on holidays. Hiltons closed in the early 1980s, and the site is now occupied by Robert Dyas. The bus in the far distance is approximately where the shopping area finished (as it does today); beyond it is the distant horizon of the surrounding countryside.

Victoria Park c1950
H252007

Note the hedge which shields people in the park from the noise and dust from the busy A272 (South Road). Notice, too, the couple walking towards the camera in the centre of the photograph. It must have been a hot and sunny day, because the man is wearing shorts (though still keeping his dignity with his long socks and a jacket), whilst that woman would not wish to be seen without her hat.

Victoria Park c1960 H252048

Richard Pannett was a carpenter, builder and businessman who lived in Church Road. He bought a five-acre meadow in 1878, and a further two-acre wood in 1897; the two plots were then sold to the District Council for £3000, and duly named Victoria Park as a memorial to the Diamond Jubilee. This photograph gives an indication of the size of the park - Haywards Heath is very lucky to have such an amenity. The pitched roof on the far right is the lych-gate to St Wilfrid's church, and a few of the larger tombstones can just be detected to the extreme right. The level area in the foreground has been sculpted from the landscape to form a pitch for Haywards Heath's football team, but you will have to get here before kick-off if you want a seat!

*Victoria Park, the
Paddling Pool c1960*
H252042

This was very popular with
young children as they
splashed around under the
watchful eye of an adult.
Tennis was also catered for
(and still is) in another area
of this extensive park. The
central location is easily
accessible to all. The mature
oak trees give plenty of
shade, and they thrive on
the heavy clay soil that is
typically found throughout
the surrounding area. The
oak is often described as
'Sussex weed'.

The Park c1960 H252037

Some parts of Victoria Park were left as woodland, and bracken, silver birch and oak thrive. It would be difficult to guess from the photograph that this was in the centre of a town. The woodland is host to a wide variety of wildlife, though there are no rare examples.

Victoria Park and St Wilfrid's Church c1960 H252031

This is one of the best views of St Wilfrid's, framed in this photograph by the straight trunks of the larch trees. The mound on which these trees were planted was created from the excavated soil from the railway tunnel; the track runs along a deep cutting alongside the park to the left of this view. The sound of trains can be heard whilst walking in this area of the park. St Wilfrid's was built between 1862 and 1865. The site is very near where a windmill once stood in the previous century, though it was long gone before the building of the church. In 1863, the cornerstone was laid on St Wilfrid's day (12 October), and the church was completed just two years later, though it had a very small graveyard and no clock. The graveyard was extended in 1888, whilst the clock did not arrive until 1921. It was the town's peace memorial, and was inaugurated on Empire Day (24 May).

◄ *Muster Green c1950*
H252583

Muster Green is triangular in plan, as we can see from this photograph. The A272 is the right-hand road, with St Wilfrid's church in the distance, whilst the left-hand road leads to the junction with Boltro Road and further on, over the railway, reaches the Broadway. There are a large number of pollarded trees on Muster Green at this date.

◀ *Boltro Road c1960* H252035

There are a number of unusual features in this road, not least the name! It is thought that it might derive from 'Bolla's tree', but who Bolla was or when he lived is open to speculation. It is also possible that the name derives from 'bull's trough'. This is a slightly more logical reason, because the cattle auction was at the end of the road, next to the railway station, and water for the livestock would be available from troughs, which were provided not just in the immediate vicinity, but along the drove-ways as well. The brick classical-style building in the centre of the photograph is the old post office (it moved into the Orchards shopping centre in the early 1980s). Today, Boltro Road has a mix of commercial businesses and housing. Some of the businesses are in large multi-occupied office blocks on the right of the road, whilst opposite are houses; some date back to the Edwardian period (100 years ago), while some are more recent. The latest development is Charter Gate, a complex of apartments on the site of the old police station - some of its architectural features have been retained from the 19th-century building. It can be seen from the railway station, which is where our tour of Haywards Heath began.

◀ *The Memorial Stone c1960* H252057

At the western apex of Muster Green is the war memorial, a 7.5 ton Cornish granite slab, which was unveiled in 1921 (the same year as the church clock) - both ceremonies were performed by Lord Leconsfield. The memorial bears 167 names. It is interesting to compare the height of the hedge with the one in photograph H252583 (page 44). This site is always a focal point each 11 November, when the fallen of all conflicts are duly remembered.

45

◀ *The Library c1960* H252055

The library is to be found in Boltro Road, which leads off Muster Green towards the railway station. It is built on land owned by the Urban District Council and on land adjacent to the main offices of the council at Oaklands, the former home of Sir James Bradford. The library building has recently undergone a substantial extension, built in the same style as the building shown in the photograph. It is a much used and valued facility for everyone.

▲ *Muster Green c1950* H252585

Muster Green is another open space maintained by the local council, and it flanks the A272. The name is said to originate from the mustering of troops during the English Civil War in the 17th century, but it could equally originate from a much earlier 13th-century charter allowing animals to be gathered (mustered) for two annual fairs in April and November, with a special mention that pigs could be mustered. Markets and fairs have always played an important part throughout the country, and Haywards Heath is no exception. The road heading into the distance is Boltro Road, which leads down to the railway station - the railway line is off to the right of this photograph.

◄ *The Sergison Arms c1960* H252034

Within sight of the war memorial stands the Sergison Arms, the oldest pub in Haywards Heath: it dates from the 16th century, when it was the home of John Vynall (who died in 1599). It became an inn in the 18th century, when it was called the Dolphin, possibly because dolphins form part of the Sergison family's coat of arms. The inn was renamed the Sergison Arms in 1845, but it reverted back to the Dolphin during the 1990s when the premises were remodelled and upgraded to modern standards. It is certainly a very popular and attractive venue.

THE VILLAGES

LINDFIELD, *The Common c1960* L221076

Just a couple of miles from Haywards Heath railway station is the attractive and ancient village of Lindfield, named after the lime (or linden) trees which flank the village High Street. Though it is not apparent in this photograph, the Common was (and still is) used for variety of sporting activities, football and cricket being particularly popular. The Common is much appreciated by the local residents.

► **LINDFIELD**
*The Cricket Pavilion
c1960* L221123

Alas, the pavilion is no longer here. It overlooked the Common, where the local cricket team often played exciting matches. A local Lindfield family hold a unique place in the history of cricket: the players Fred Tate (1867-1943) and his son Maurice (1895-1956) are the only father and son to have represented England against Australia.

◄ **LINDFIELD**
The Common c1955
L221036

The row of houses
overlooking the Common are
certainly in a prime location,
though today the road is
considerably busier. Notice
on the extreme right of the
photograph a short white
post; and then look at
photograph L221074, page
52-53.

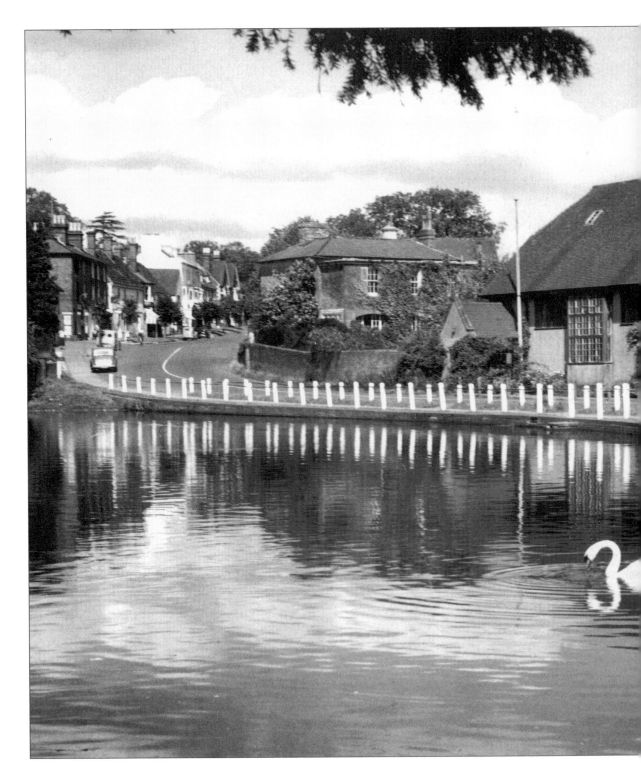

LINDFIELD
The Pond c1960 L221074

The row of white posts form an attractive (and safe) barrier at the pond's edge. There are local stories of stagecoaches driving into the water before the posts were erected to cool their wheels. Overlooking the pond is King Edward Hall, opened in 1911 and designed by Walter Tower. The scene has hardly changed today.

▼ **LINDFIELD,** *High Street c1960* L221110

The pond, which is basically circular, is situated at the southern end of the High Street, with the Common beyond. Not seen in this photograph are cottages and houses off to the right that overlook the pond - their gardens front directly onto it. The large house on the left with the shuttered windows stands on a busy road junction, and the sign pointing left indicates the route to Scaynes Hill, Chailey and Lewes.

▶ **LINDFIELD**
Post Office Corner c1955
L221038

The chequered brick and weather boarded cottage (right) is Barclays Bank; it opened in 1910 in what was then the front room of a cottage. The bank was to stay here until 1999. The post office is in the adjacent building off to the right of the photograph. These buildings give a cottage feel to what is essentially a commercial street, as we can see from the buildings opposite - they house a shop, a pub and the outbuildings of a brewery. The large black poplar tree in the centre of the photograph was cut down in 1962, as it had become a hazard.

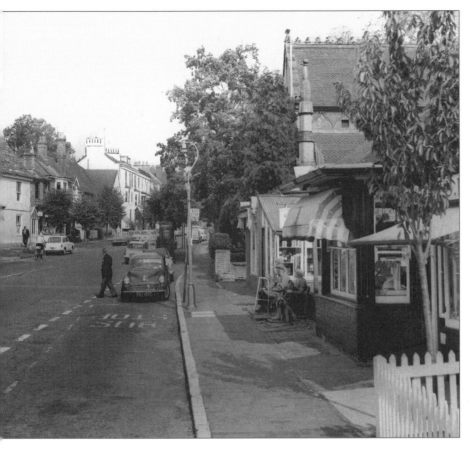

◀ **LINDFIELD**
High Street c1965
L221133

On the extreme left is Lloyds Bank, whilst next door is the Stand Up Inn, so called because of the lack of seating - this ensured that any lunchtime customers were not late back to their workplace! The white-fronted building further along was once part of the Durrant brewery, and later the home of the Wireless Museum, which displayed a wide range of fascinating instruments that were lovingly cared for by Ray Letworthy. Unfortunately, owing to health reasons, the museum closed in 1999. The butcher's shop on the extreme right is H J Box; the family owned grazing lands nearby, which enabled them to sell their high-quality meat locally.

▶ **LINDFIELD**
High Street c1960
L221112

The hanging sign on the extreme left is that of the Stand Up Inn, whilst further along on the opposite side of the road is another pub, the Red Lion, which was originally a well used coaching inn - it was easily seen with its large projecting hanging sign.

LINDFIELD
High Street c1960 L221115

Opposite the Red Lion (right), whose projecting hanging sign has long been a feature of the High Street, is another long-established family business. Richard Humphries bought an existing bakery in 1875, when he was just 20 years old. He died in 1940, after being the village baker for 55 years. Subsequent owners have retained the name as well the quality of the goods, and queuing for the freshly baked bread and cakes has become a tradition, especially on a Saturday morning!

▶ **LINDFIELD**
High Street c1960 L221071

Dating from the 1500s (and possibly earlier), the half-timbered building on the left fronting both the High Street and Hickmans Lane has had a chequered history. It was used as commercial offices before Miss Maud Savill, daughter of the local shipping magnate Walter Savill, paid for its restoration; it then became one of the most photographed houses in the High Street. The Savill family home was Finches, a sprawling house situated along Hickmans Lane, with grounds that were tended by twelve full-time gardeners. At the time when this photograph was taken, the house was a country hotel; this was later to be demolished and the land used for a housing estate. The building on the opposite corner is currently an antiques shop, one of a number in the High Street.

◀ **LINDFIELD**
Finches Park Road c1960 L221091

These detached houses are part of the Finches development, with no trace of the original house remaining. Note how the grass verges between pavement and roadway help to create a sense of space, especially as the planning incorporated the existing mature trees.

▲ **LINDFIELD,** *High Street c1955* L221052

In 1920, a lit candle almost destroyed the Bent Arms hotel and pub (right); luckily, the local fire brigade acted quickly. Named after a local dignitary, Dr Bent, it advertises itself with the attractive heraldic hanging sign projecting well into the High Street, whilst the hotel proudly exhibits an AA sign with its black lettering on a distinctive yellow background. Motorcars were becoming more attainable in the 1950s, and such hotels were extremely popular with travellers visiting the area for either business or pleasure.

◄**LINDFIELD**
High Street, Looking South c1955
L221039

The house on the right dates from the 16th century, as we can see from the timbers in the gable end. The front was updated during the 18th century, and during the 19th century, it was the home of Dr Richard Tupper, who entertained his guests in style. They included Charles Dickens, who stayed here on several occasions. Notice the different levels of the buildings on each side of the road: the ones on the western side are elevated and protected by a grass strip from the road. The Bent Arms sign (left) is easily recognisable, and would have no doubt been a welcome sight to tired travellers.

LINDFIELD
The Bower House and the Church c1955 L221060

The High Street starts to curve its way around the church, and motorists were no doubt aided by the solid white line in the middle of the road. The Bower House on the left is quintessentially a Sussex-style house with its attractive tile-hung upper elevation and small dormer windows in the roof space. Opposite is a smaller terraced house boasting a large hanging sign, 'Formerly the Tiger', which had been another pub up until 1916.

LINDFIELD, *All Saints' Church c1960* L221064

All Saints' dates from the 13th century; the present building was extensively refurbished in the 19th century, and the stained glass windows by Charles Kempe are particularly important. The war memorial is quite rightly in a prominent position, and was unveiled on 12 May 1922.

LINDFIELD, *Old Place, the West Wing c1955* L221016

Adjacent to a thatched cottage said to date from 1390, this 1590s building was the farmhouse of Townlands Farm.
In 1875 Charles Kempe, the stained glass window designer, bought the property.

LINDFIELD
Pretty Corner c1960
L221062

These eye-catching houses are situated on the bend of the road and opposite All Saints' church. The house on the left has a Horsham stone roof; note how the larger stones are placed near the eaves, whilst the sizes diminish nearer the top of the roof. The brick chimneystacks add a degree of grandeur to the profile of these much-photographed houses. No wonder this is called Pretty Corner, a name still used today.

LINDFIELD, *Old Place c1955* L221013

After buying the farmhouse of Townlands Farm in 1875, Charles Kempe promptly began to enlarge the property in a style in keeping with the existing small house. The property was renamed Old Place, with the original building called West Wing. The decorated column in the garden is a sundial, said to be a copy of the one at Pembroke College, Oxford where Kempe studied. On the top of the sundial is a pelican feeding her young, symbolically representing piety. Sir David Hunt, who in 1977 won the television programme 'Mastermind', lived here.

▲ LINDFIELD

The Tudor Barn, the Mill and the Railway c1955 L221018

Situated on the River Ouse and known as the Deans' Mill, this was an active mill used for grinding corn. By the mid 1930s it was in a dilapidated state, but it was bought by a Mr and Mrs Horsefield, who renovated the building. By 1937 it was again grinding corn, and Mr Horsefield sold his own brand of wholemeal flour. He was an engineer, and he then decided to create the miniature steam train track around the grounds. It proved a great success, as we can see here, and brought much enjoyment to many generations of children.

◄ *detail of L221018*

▼ **LINDFIELD,** *The Tudor Barn c1955* L221024

Mrs Horsefield was just as enterprising as her husband; she opened a meat-free restaurant in Haywards Heath, which became very popular. Her next enterprise was to convert the adjacent Elizabethan barn into a tearoom, which gave adults the chance to keep an eye on the children whilst also catching up with the latest news. In this photograph, business seems to be brisk! By the mid 1970s, the mill had stopped working, and the both the mill and barn are now private residences.

▶ **LINDFIELD**
Paxhill c1955 L221059

The house was built in 1595 by Ninien Boord (his father had been court jester to King Henry VIII). The extensive estate was used by Canadian troops during World War II. Part of the estate was later to become a golf course with exhilarating views of the surrounding countryside and attractive villages.

◄ ARDINGLY
High Street c1955
A207036

Invariably the village shop and post office (left) was the social hub of village life, and Ardingly is no exception. The boy on his bicycle is probably calculating to see if his pocket money would be enough to buy the latest toy on display in the window. Ardingly hosts the South of England Show, an important agricultural event with livestock competitions and horse jumping, and has often been visited by members of the royal family.

► ARDINGLY
The Gardeners Arms c1955 A207023

The pub sells Tamplins beer (a Brighton-based brewery). Its name is rather apt, as the village is just a couple of miles south of Wakehurst, an extensive estate under the care of the National Trust, and also the outpost of the Royal Botanical Gardens, whose headquarters are at Kew. The gardens are a blaze of colour, particularly in spring and autumn, and it is the home of the Millennium Seed Bank Project. Though the pub still exits today (2004), it is now considerably larger than it is in this photograph. The road has also been re-aligned, and the pub is now further away from the road.

◄ **BALCOMBE**
The Village c1955
B503006

Unlike the other villages that are mentioned in this book, Balcombe has a railway station, and it has undergone a considerable change since this photograph, though some buildings are still recognisable. An antique chandelier and fireplace shop is now where the Balcombe Stores were.

◀ ARDINGLY
The College
c1960 A207054

To the south of Ardingly is Ardingly College, a public school with a good academic record. This view has changed very little. Alumni include Eddie Izzard, the cross-dressing comedian, and Michael Fish, the weather forecaster. The college is a landmark that is easily seen from southbound trains crossing the Great Ouse viaduct between Balcombe and Haywards Heath.

◀ WHITEMANS GREEN
Brook Street c1955 W452001

On the approach into Cuckfield from Balcombe is Whitemans Green. Being on higher ground, this was to have been the site of the local church, but as soon as any building work was started, it had been destroyed by the following morning. The puzzled residents duly stayed awake all night to -establish the cause. They did not have to wait long, as a very tall and angry ghostly figure bathed head-to-toe in a white light appeared and threw the building stones down the hill. They then named the area after that ghostly figure!

WHITEMANS GREEN
The Village c1965
W452011

Whitemans Green is a small hamlet that today has now been absorbed into Cuckfield. The village sign shown on the right of the photograph depicts a cuckoo, a rebus for Cuckfield, whilst the village stores (left) were a branch of Spar and also housed the local post office.

CUCKFIELD, *High Street c1950* C426004

Before the main A23 road was built, Cuckfield was busy with horse-drawn coaches on their way between London and Brighton. Visually, this scene is virtually unchanged today. The main road (A272) ran through Cuckfield, and turns right at the junction beyond the parked car, whilst the minor northbound road to Whitemans Green continues into the distance up the hill. Today, through traffic uses the 1989 bypass to the south of the village, thereby creating an air of calm, not too unlike the atmosphere in the photograph.

CUCKFIELD
Broad Street c1950
C426019

At this road junction is the Cuckfield branch of J W Upton (the Haywards Heath furniture store), next to Lloyds Bank (right). The attractive clock still survives, which is just as well, as the building is called Clock House. Broad Street leads off into the distance, and is the main route to Haywards Heath.

CUCKFIELD, *The Clock, High Street c1950* C426002

On the right of the photograph are various businesses, including Barclays Bank, a tobacconist, a hardware store and a dairy. Antique shops, estate agents and a sub-post office can now be found here.

CUCKFIELD
High Street c1965
C426022

Two doors from D P Gowen (selling clothes for ladies and gentlemen, left) are International Stores, selling food and general provisions. Local delivery of purchases by bicycle could still have been available at this time, though the bicycle in front of the shop appears to be a customer's, as there is no large basket frame noticeable.

◄ **CUCKFIELD**
*Holy Trinity Church
c1950* C426011

The church dates from the
13th century and is built
of local stone. The wood-
shingled spire was
destroyed by fire in 1980
and a new spire was
completed in 1981, but
many residents miss the
original eight-sided spire
we see in this photograph.
The interior is a delight,
particularly the painted
ceiling by Charles Kempe
that dates from the late
1880s.

◀ **CUCKFIELD**
Church Cottages c1950 C426005

In 1924, a Miss Maberley died, leaving her three dilapidated churchyard cottages to the then vicar for use by the local poor and needy. The vicar could not afford to keep the cottages, and the Church Commissioners sanctioned their sale to the then tenants, much to the annoyance of a local entrepreneur, who wanted to demolish the cottages and re-use the old timbers.

◀ **CUCKFIELD**
South Street c1950
C426001

The King's Head pub proudly advertises Tamplins beer (a Brighton-based brewery), together with an RAC badge over the door. This indicated that accommodation was available here, and that the rooms were of a standard approved by the Royal Automobile Club. The stone trough on the left of the photograph is a reminder that horses and cattle were often driven through Cuckfield.

CUCKFIELD
The White Harte c1950
C426009

Having just passed the
White Harte, the car may
well be calling in at the
petrol station for fuel, where
the attendant would
operate the Shell petrol
pump. We can also see Shell
advertising on the wall.
The garage is now a private
house, whilst the White
Harte is still welcoming
customers who need their
own preferred type of fuel!

▶ **CUCKFIELD**
Ockenden Manor
c1960 C426037

This is an ironmaster's house, built in the early 17th century; it was the home of the Burrell family (whose heraldic device is shown in mosaic on the Burrell Arms pub opposite Haywards Heath railway station). Today it is a hotel and restaurant from which the extensive grounds can be viewed.

◀ **CUCKFIELD PARK**
c1960 C426036

Cuckfield Park was built by Henry Bower, a wealthy ironmaster, who died in 1588 and was buried in Holy Trinity church. The house is not open to the public. The avenue of trees was damaged during the 1987 storm, and specimens were duly replaced. Cuckfield Park is still a landmark from the A272, the road that leads to the village of Bolney.

▲ **BOLNEY,** *Main Street 1957* B507041

Agriculture was the dominant employer in the area, and this was often reflected in village life and facilities - note the tractor on the right of the photograph. Ancillary businesses included a newsagent, a butcher, a baker and the post office (where the white van is parked), as well as the builder R O Ayres, who proudly advertises his telephone number on his van (foreground) in the hope of attracting new customers. The tower of the church of St Mary Magdalene can be seen behind the houses on the left.

◀**BOLNEY**
Bolney Court c1955
B507025

This house was originally called Gravenhurst. During World War II British soldiers camped in the grounds, whilst the house was used by a London-based engineering company whose premises had been bombed. The building was then used as a home for blind people, and renamed Bolney Court. In 1955, at the time of this photograph, it became a school for emotionally disturbed children and was re-named Farley Close.

▲ *detail of B507050*

◀**BOLNEY**
The Post Office 1957
B507050

Only the post office is still here, and it too is under threat of closure. Opposite in the 1950s was Payne Transport, a family-run business which also had depots in nearby Handcross and Brighton. The business eventually closed upon the retirement of Alec Payne (a grandson of the founders) in 2000.

◄ **BOLNEY**
The Lych Gate c1955 B507002

The lych gate was built in 1905 and paid for by Edward Huth in memory of his parents, who moved to Wykehurst House in the 1860s. A new house designed by Edward Barry (son of Charles Barry, architect of the Houses of Parliament) was built in 1874. The lych gate was damaged by a falling yew during the 1987 storm.

◄ **BOLNEY**
The Brighton Road and Ye Olde Tudor House c1955
B507031

The A23 passes just to the east of Bolney. With the decline of agriculture, farmland and buildings were used for different purposes, and Fords Farm became the Tudor Tea Rooms, a welcome stopping-off point for passing travellers. In the 1960s it grew and was named the Bolney Stage, inferring that it could have been an old coaching inn. Today it is a restaurant, and stands to the north of the 1960s flyover across the A272, which leads back to Haywards Heath.

► **CHAILEY**
The Village Green c1965
C437004

About five miles east of Haywards Heath (and halfway to Lewes) is Chailey, a scattered village whose centre is shown in the photographs. The house on the left is later in date than its neighbour, with its distinctive Sussex-style half-tiled elevations and attic rooms. The tiles would probably have been made from the local clay, as Chailey was also known for its own type of pottery (dating from the 1600s to early 1800s): it was earthenware glazed with a dark brown slip, and subsequently decorated with suitable inscriptions in pale yellow dots and lines. There are examples of Chailey pottery on display at the Brighton Museum and Art Gallery.

◄ CHAILEY
The Village c1965 C437006

Chailey (thought to mean 'clearing in the gorse') is a village that straddles the A272. The village stores are next to the telephone box (centre right), and though the buildings still exist, today's motorist probably passes them without a second look. This is because on the left about a quarter of a mile away is the entrance to Chailey Heritage, the nationally recognized school for handicapped children, whilst on the opposite side of the road is Chailey Common with its windmill (supposedly sited at the geographical centre of the county of Sussex). Just to the north of Chailey is the terminus for the well-known Bluebell Railway, a steam train ride through the Sussex countryside, which is very popular with visitors of all ages.

BUS
STOP

SCAYNES HILL
The Anchor Inn c1955
S474004

Mid-way between Chailey and Haywards Heath is Scaynes Hill, and this photograph shows the summit of the hill. Though there is still a pub here, it is now called the Farmers. Opposite it there is now a large petrol station, as well as a road junction that leads onto the Common. The village is certainly on a hill, and at the foot of the hill is a small vineyard, as well as a thriving family-owned garden centre. These are just two examples of the many varied businesses that are established in and around Scaynes Hill.

◀ **SCAYNES HILL**
The Post Office c1960
S474038

The post office and general stores are still at the same site today at the summit of the hill and near the crossroads (though the proprietors have changed). Today the road traffic is much busier, so pedestrian-operated traffic lights are now installed here. The road junction to the right leads to the Common.

◀ SCAYNES HILL
The Village c1960 S474045

Looking westwards towards Haywards Heath, this view is virtually unchanged today. Beyond the houses on the right-hand side of the road is the village recreation ground complete with its new Millennium village hall, a welcome amenity for the residents of Scaynes Hill. The figure in the photograph may well be returning home from her visit to the local shop.

◀ SCAYNES HILL
The Common c1955
S474018

We have just passed St Augustine's church and are heading away from the village. The speed restriction sign would allow the motorist to savour the open road, travelling though the attractive country lanes that criss-cross this rural part of Sussex. The view has changed little.

SCAYNES HILL, *Nash Lane and Butterbox c1955* S474016

Thank goodness for signposts, as they were (and still are) a necessity when travelling though these rural areas. Originally made of wood, later versions were metal, and visually the black lettering certainly stands out from the white-painted pointing board. Note that no distances are indicated to either Dane Hill or Horsted Keynes - perhaps it was felt that it was not that important! No doubt the local postman would know, as there would probably be a daily collection even from this rather isolated spot.

INDEX

NAMES OF SUBSCRIBERS

The following people have kindly supported this book by subscribing to copies before publication.

Age Concern, Haywards Heath

The Archer Family, Haywards Heath

Gillian & Derek Archer, Haywards Heath

Mr & Mrs R G Batchelor and family

John Beaumont, Haywards Heath

D W Bellingham

Adrien & Michaela Bischoff-Dyson, Haywards Heath

Roy Bliss

Mr & Mrs P W Blunden - 'Many Past Happy Memories'

Bob & Trish of Haywards Heath

Alfred & Jenny Bodimeade, Lindfield

Mr C & Mrs H Braybon

Geoffrey W Breading, Haywards Heath born and bred

Mrs S A Brigden, Haywards Heath

Richard N Brooks, WWII baby in Delney Ave

Sam & Allan Brown Family, Haywards Heath

Shane T Brown, Haywards Heath

Graham James Butler

Ian Cains, Haywards Heath

In loving memory of John Carthy

Mr & Mrs P J Chadwick, Haywards Heath

Alan D Chambers

Chris Chapman, Lindfield

Mr & Mrs P Clark, Haywards Heath

Sue Clarke, Brian Coomber, Haywards Heath

In memory of Royston Clarke, Haywards Heath

The Cliff Family, Haywards Heath

Mr & Mrs J Clink, Haywards Heath

Mr T D & Mrs J Coleman, Haywards Heath

James & Thomas Colins, Haywards Heath

Mr Philip Cook & Mrs Edna Cook, Haywards Heath

Ray Costick, Haywards Heath

In memory of Victoria Coughlan (Nye)

Mrs J & Mr L Cruttenden, Haywards Heath

The Cunningham Family, Lindfield

J D Dann, Haywards Heath

In memory of F W Davey

The Davey Family, Haywards Heath

The Denyer Family, Haywards Heath

Gay Duffy, Haywards Heath

The Ellis Family, Lindfield

Mr P & Mrs E Elphick, Haywards Heath

Mr J & Mrs G Elphick, Haywards Heath

Dave Evans and the Evans Family of Haywards Heath

The Evans Family, Haywards Heath

David Everitt, Haywards Heath

Brian Farmer

Jo & Trevor Fisher

Thomas William Fox, born 13/09/04

Mr A & Mrs V Fruin, Lindfield

Mr A & Mrs S Fruin, Lindfield

Family of Maurice & Frances Fuller, Haywards Heath

The Funnell Family of Haywards Heath

Clive & Enid Gallewicz, Haywards Heath

The Goodchild Family, Haywards Heath

John Hall

In memory of Owen Hall, Cuckfield

Irene Hallett, Haywards Heath

In memory of Pat Hanna, Haywards Heath

Colin Harris & Jane Gibson

The Head Family

Andrew Heighton, Haywards Heath

Rodney S Henry

Shayne Hilbourne, Haywards Heath

The Holland Family, Haywards Heath

For my late husband Huburt who loved the town

Anne Hurst

The Ingebretson Family, Cuckfield

The Jarvis Family, Haywards Heath

The Jellett Family of Lindfield

Alan R Jenkins, Haywards Heath

Cnty Cllr. Mrs Margaret Johnson DL

The Jones Family of Finches Park Road, Lindfield

The Jones Family, Lindfield

Ray Jones, Lindfield

The Joyner Family, Haywards Heath

The Judd Family, Lindfield

The Kernohan Family, Haywards Heath

Mr Robin F Lacey

Maggie Lamb, Haywards Heath

The Leather Family, Haywards Heath

Robert & Joy Madgwick, Haywards Heath

Lavinia Malins, Lindfield

Zoë & Chéri Maskell; wonderful daughters

Mr C & Mrs D Mason, Haywards Heath

Ms M Mason, Burgess Hill

John Merrett, Haywards Heath

To Christine Moon with love from Gordon

Mr & Mrs R Moon, Butler's Green

Eileen & John Morgan, Lindfield

The Mundy Family, Haywards Heath

Graham & Janet Mundy, Haywards Heath

David & Emma Neate, Haywards Heath

The Nelson Family, Haywards Heath

Roger Newnham, Haywards Heath

Tim Nias, Happy Birthday, 20th November

Andrew Osborne, Haywards Heath

The Palmer Family, Lindfield

Mr R & Mrs K Pannett

John A Park, Haywards Heath

Darren Ian Parker, Haywards Heath

David Ian Parker, Haywards Heath

Mrs S Parkes, Mr D Parkes, Haywards Heath

Andrew Parsons, Perth, Western Australia

G E Pattenden

Mark Graham Pattenden

The Pedder Family, Haywards Heath

Frank Penfold

Patrick Penfold

Jenefer Penny

Mr D & Mrs G Pickett, Haywards Heath

Mr M & Mrs C Porter, Fradley

Mr & Mrs Powell, Haywards Heath

Ernest L Poyle, Haywards Heath

Mr & Mrs P Price

P F Pullinger, Haywards Heath

M A Puttock, Haywards Heath

The Robertson Family, Haywards Heath

Kathleen & Eddie Rogan, Haywards Heath

Lilian Rogers, Haywards Heath

The Rumsey Family, Haywards Heath

M C Rumsey, Haywards Heath 1967

The Lee Smith Family, Cuckfield

In memory of Allen & Mary Smith

The Smith Family, Haywards Heath

Mr A H & Mrs P Snape, Haywards Heath

Jayne & Mark Sorge, Haywards Heath

Malcolm & Pauline Springall, Lindfield

Sheila Staerck, Lindfield, Sussex

Vic & Audrey Stevens, Haywards Heath

The Swiggs Family, Haywards Heath

The Thomson Family, Haywards Heath

Claire Timms, Haywards Heath

As a tribute to my Dad, Charles Tucker

Patrick R Tucker, Haywards Heath

David J Tucker, Haywards Heath

Alan G Tuddenham, Haywards Heath (1946-54)

Mr & Mrs Turner, Haywards Heath

The Vivash & Corton Family, Haywards Heath

Mr H G T Walter, Haywards Heath

Mr Darren M Weller, Haywards Heath

Tony & Bridget Weller of Haywards Heath

P & M Wells, Haywards Heath

Mr & Mrs G Went, Lindfield

Frank & Rita Willett, Haywards Heath

John B Wilson, Haywards Heath

Stanley & Winifred Wilton

The Wood Family, Haywards Heath

The Woodhams Family

FRITH PRODUCTS & SERVICES

Francis Frith would doubtless be pleased to know that the pioneering publishing venture he started in 1860 still continues today. Over a hundred and forty years later, The Francis Frith Collection continues in the same innovative tradition and is now one of the foremost publishers of vintage photographs in the world. Some of the current activities include:

Interior Decoration

Today Frith's photographs can be seen framed and as giant wall murals in thousands of pubs, restaurants, hotels, banks, retail stores and other public buildings throughout the country. In every case they enhance the unique local atmosphere of the places they depict and provide reminders of gentler days in an increasingly busy and frenetic world.

Product Promotions

Frith products are used by many major companies to promote the sales of their own products or to reinforce their own history and heritage. Frith promotions have been used by Hovis bread, Courage beers, Scots Porage Oats, Colman's mustard, Cadbury's foods, Mellow Birds coffee, Dunhill pipe tobacco, Guinness, and Bulmer's Cider.

Genealogy and Family History

As the interest in family history and roots grows world-wide, more and more people are turning to Frith's photographs of Great Britain for images of the towns, villages and streets where their ancestors lived; and, of course, photographs of the churches and chapels where their ancestors were christened, married and buried are an essential part of every genealogy tree and family album.

Frith Products

All Frith photographs are available Framed or just as Mounted Prints and Posters (size 23 x 16 inches). These may be ordered from the address below. From time to time other products - Address Books, Calendars, Table Mats, etc - are available.

The Internet

Already fifty thousand Frith photographs can be viewed and purchased on the internet through the Frith websites and a myriad of partner sites.

For more detailed information on Frith companies and products, look at these sites:

> www.francisfrith.co.uk
> www.francisfrith.com
> *(for North American visitors)*

See the complete list of Frith Books at:

www.francisfrith.co.uk

This web site is regularly updated with the latest list of publications from the Frith Book Company. If you wish to buy books relating to another part of the country that your local bookshop does not stock, you may purchase on-line.

For further information, trade, or author enquiries please contact us at the address below:
The Francis Frith Collection, Frith's Barn, Teffont, Salisbury, Wiltshire, England SP3 5QP.
Tel: +44 (0)1722 716 376 Fax: +44 (0)1722 716 881 Email: sales@francisfrith.co.uk

See Frith books on the internet at www.francisfrith.co.uk

FREE PRINT OF YOUR CHOICE

Mounted Print
Overall size 14 x 11 inches (355 x 280mm)

Choose any Frith photograph in this book.
Simply complete the Voucher opposite and return it with your remittance for £2.25 (to cover postage and handling) and we will print the photograph of your choice in SEPIA (size 11 x 8 inches) and supply it in a cream mount with a burgundy rule line (overall size 14 x 11 inches).
Please note: photographs with a reference number starting with a "Z" are not Frith photographs and cannot be supplied under this offer.
Offer valid for delivery to one UK address only.

PLUS: Order additional Mounted Prints at HALF PRICE - £7.49 each (normally £14.99)
If you would like to order more Frith prints from this book, possibly as gifts for friends and family, you can buy them at half price (with no additional postage and handling costs).

PLUS: Have your Mounted Prints framed
For an extra £14.95 per print you can have your mounted print(s) framed in an elegant polished wood and gilt moulding, overall size 16 x 13 inches (no additional postage and handling required).

IMPORTANT!

These special prices are only available if you use this form to order . You must use the ORIGINAL VOUCHER on this page (no copies permitted). We can only despatch to one UK address. This offer cannot be combined with any other offer.

Send completed Voucher form to:
The Francis Frith Collection, Frith's Barn, Teffont, Salisbury, Wiltshire SP3 5QP

CHOOSE A PHOTOGRAPH FROM THIS BOOK

Voucher for **FREE** and Reduced Price Frith Prints

Please do not photocopy this voucher. Only the original is valid, so please fill it in, cut it out and return it to us with your order.

Picture ref no	Page no	Qty	Mounted @ £7.49	Framed + £14.95	Total Cost £
		1	Free of charge*	£	£
			£7.49	£	£
			£7.49	£	£
			£7.49	£	£
			£7.49	£	£
			£7.49	£	£

Please allow 28 days for delivery. Offer available to one UK address only

* Post & handling	£2.25
Total Order Cost	£

Title of this book . . . .
I enclose a cheque/postal order for £ . . . .
made payable to 'The Francis Frith Collection'

OR please debit my Mastercard / Visa / Maestro / Amex card, details below

Card Number

Issue No (Maestro only)   Valid from (Maestro)

Expires   Signature

Name Mr/Mrs/Ms . . . .
Address . . . .
. . . .
. . . .
. . . . Postcode . . . .
Daytime Tel No . . . .
Email . . . .

Valid to 31/12/07

Would you like to find out more about Francis Frith?

We have recently recruited some entertaining speakers who are happy to visit local groups, clubs and societies to give an illustrated talk documenting Frith's travels and photographs. If you are a member of such a group and are interested in hosting a presentation, we would love to hear from you.

Our speakers bring with them a small selection of our local town and county books, together with sample prints. They are happy to take orders. A small proportion of the order value is donated to the group who have hosted the presentation. The talks are therefore an excellent way of fundraising for small groups and societies.

Can you help us with information about any of the Frith photographs in this book?

We are gradually compiling an historical record for each of the photographs in the Frith archive. It is always fascinating to find out the names of the people shown in the pictures, as well as insights into the shops, buildings and other features depicted.

If you recognize anyone in the photographs in this book, or if you have information not already included in the author's caption, do let us know. We would love to hear from you, and will try to publish it in future books or articles.

Our production team

Frith books are produced by a small dedicated team at offices in the converted Grade II listed 18th-century barn at Teffont near Salisbury, illustrated above. Most have worked with the Frith Collection for many years. All have in common one quality: they have a passion for the Frith Collection. The team is constantly expanding, but currently includes:

Paul Baron, Phillip Brennan, Jason Buck, John Buck, Ruth Butler, Heather Crisp, David Davies, Louis du Mont, Isobel Hall, Gareth Harris, Lucy Hart, Julian Hight, Peter Horne, James Kinnear, Karen Kinnear, Tina Leary, Stuart Login, David Marsh, Lesley-Ann Millard, Sue Molloy, Glenda Morgan, Wayne Morgan, Sarah Roberts, Kate Rotondetto, Dean Scource, Eliza Sackett, Terence Sackett, Sandra Sampson, Adrian Sanders, Sandra Sanger, Jan Scrivens, Julia Skinner, David Smith, Miles Smith, Lewis Taylor, Shelley Tolcher, Lorraine Tuck, Amanita Wainwright and Ricky Williams.